Emma Farrarons is a French illustrator and graphic designer. Born on the island of Cebu in the Philippines, Emma grew up in Paris. She illustrates and designs books, posters, and stationery.

She was trained in illustration at the Edinburgh College of Art and École nationale supérieure des Arts Décoratifs. She completed a textile and printmaking course at Capellagården – School of Craft and Design in Sweden and has a particular love of pattern and fabric print. She is inspired by French, Scandinavian, and Japanese design.

When she is not drawing and designing, Emma enjoys cooking, sewing, traveling, and practicing mindfulness. She lives in London with her husband and son.

Share your creations using #mindfulcoloring
See more of Emma's work on social media: @emmafarrarons

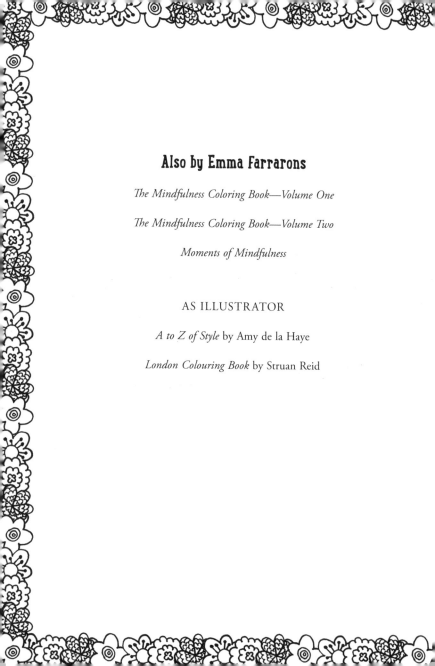

Also by Emma Farrarons

The Mindfulness Coloring Book—Volume One

The Mindfulness Coloring Book—Volume Two

Moments of Mindfulness

AS ILLUSTRATOR

A to Z of Style by Amy de la Haye

London Colouring Book by Struan Reid

THE MINDFULNESS Creativity COLORING BOOK

Anti-Stress Guided Activities in Drawing, Lettering, and Patterns

Emma Farrarons

THE EXPERIMENT

NEW YORK

THE MINDFULNESS CREATIVITY COLORING BOOK: *Anti-Stress Guided Activities in Drawing, Lettering, and Patterns*
Copyright © 2018, 2020 by Emma Farrarons

Originally published in Great Britain in 2018 as *Art of Mindfulness* by Boxtree, an imprint of Pan Macmillan, a division of Macmillan Publishers Limited. This edition published by arrangement with Pan Macmillan. First published in North America in revised form by The Experiment, LLC, in 2020.

The Experiment, LLC
220 East 23rd Street, Suite 600
New York, NY 10010-4658
theexperimentpublishing.com

This book is not intended as a substitute for the advice of a professional clinician. Readers should consult a health-care professional in all matters relating to their health and particularly with respect to any symptoms that may require diagnosis or clinical attention.

The Experiment's books are available at special discounts when purchased in bulk for premiums and sales promotions as well as for fund-raising or educational use. For details, contact us at info@theexperimentpublishing.com.

Library of Congress Cataloging-in-Publication Data is available upon request

ISBN 978-1-61519-774-3

Cover design by Beth Bugler
Cover illustrations by Emma Farrarons

Manufactured in the United States of America

First printing July 2020
10 9 8 7 6 5 4 3 2 1

For Therese Estacion

INTRODUCTION

Mindfulness meditation is all about paying attention to the present moment. Almost any activity, done right, can be an effective exercise in mindfulness and coloring in. With the gentle action of putting pen to paper, mindful coloring is well designed to help clear your mind of excess thoughts while you focus on the task at hand.

The Mindfulness Coloring series has helped a million people worldwide to find peace and calm in a busy world, with beautiful templates of patterns and peaceful scenes to adorn with color. Now, *The Mindfulness Creativity Coloring Book* goes a few steps further to offer more activities in guided creativity.

You'll find stunning scenes to color in but also motifs to repeat, drawings to complete, and handwritten lettering to practice. Offering much more than a coloring book, *The Mindfulness Creativity Coloring Book* is for you to enjoy coloring and completing in your own style.

Add more detail to the
fox's tail and color in.

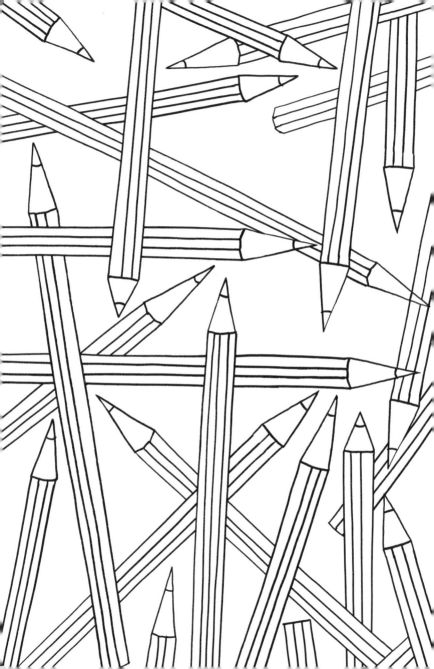

Fill in
the blank
circles.

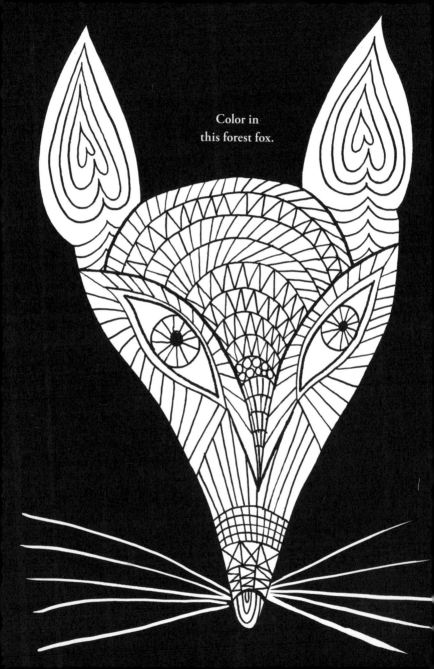

Color in
this forest fox.

Decorate this fox
with playful lines.

Trace over
these flowers.

Decorate the
roofs with color—
or patterns!

Fill this page with waves.

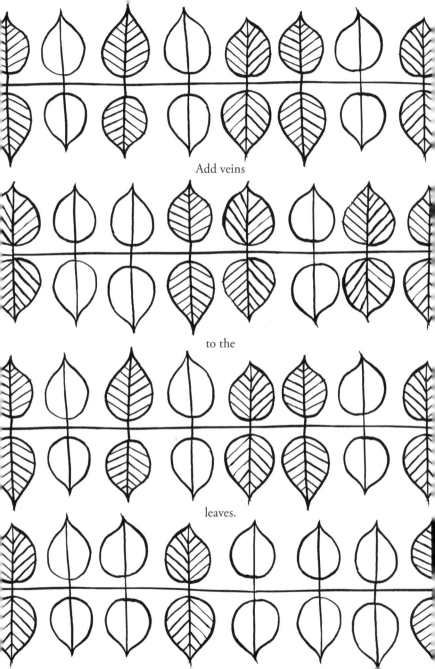

Add veins

to the

leaves.

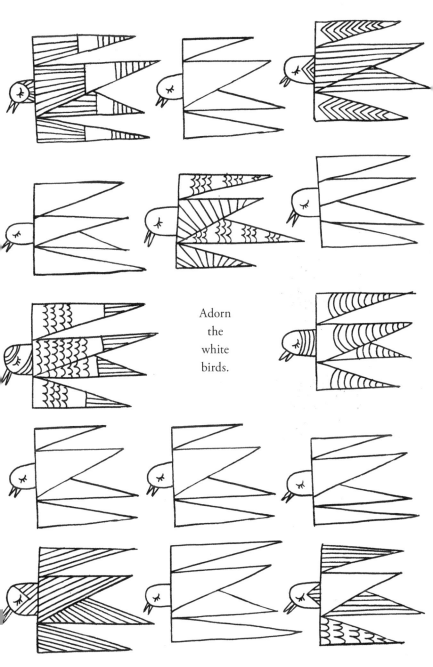

Adorn
the
white
birds.

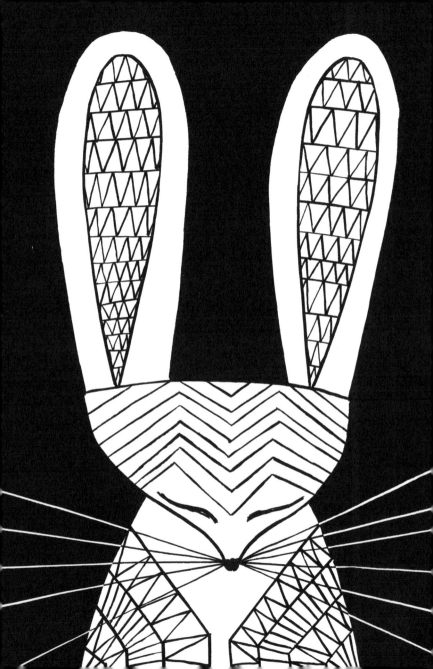

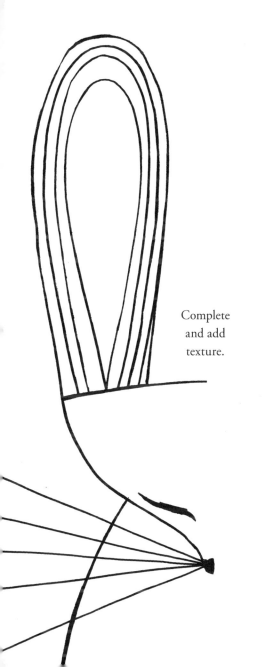

Complete
and add
texture.

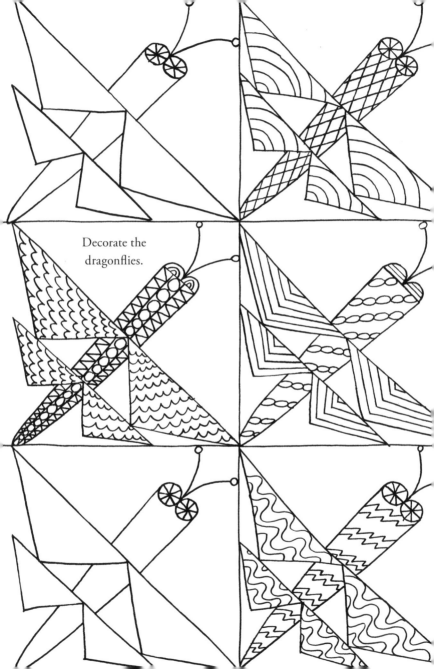

Decorate the dragonflies.

A simple, leafy, and mindful hand lettering activity

g g

h h

j i

j j

k k

l l

m m

n

o

p

g

r

s

t

𝓊 𝓊

𝓋 𝓋

𝓌 𝓌

𝓈𝒸 𝓈𝒸

𝓎 𝓎

𝓏 𝓏

tree

forest

moon

dream

air

cloud

Repeat and complete.

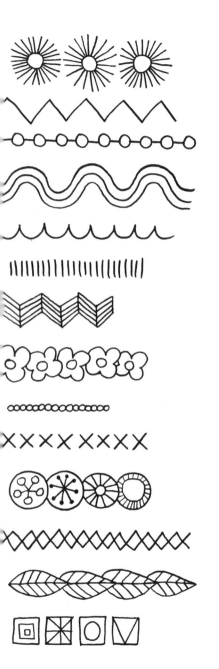

Add patterns
to the owl
and his tree.

Decorate the squirrel, moon, and stars.

What color is this squirrel?

the brighter the stars

Fyodor Dostoevsky

Repeat and complete.

Bring these
birch trees to life.

Add
detail
to the
petals.

Complete the
mountain scenery.

Create and color your own alphabet.

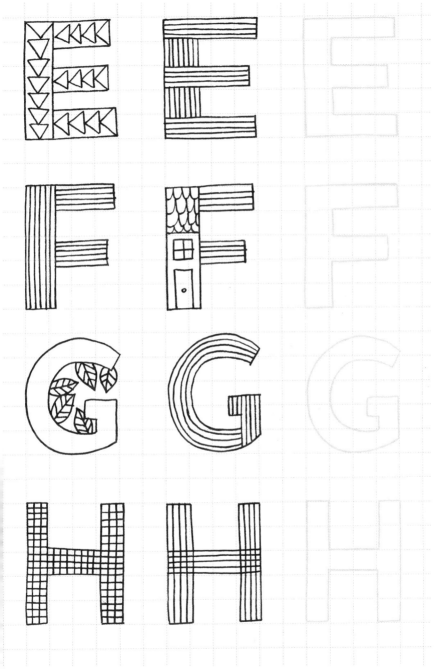

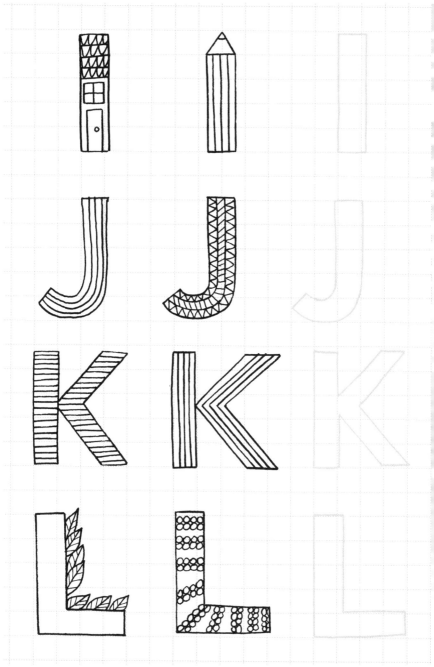

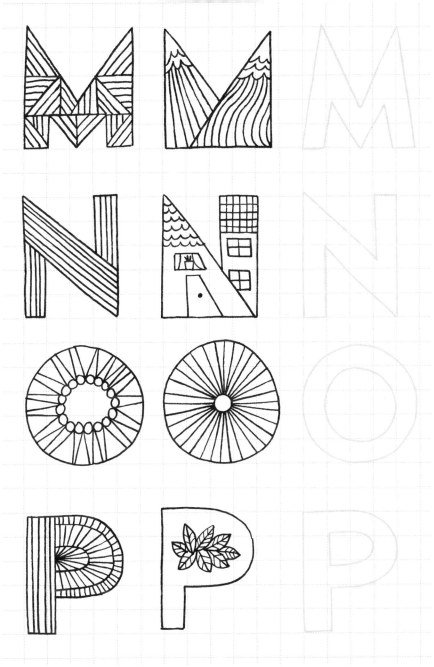

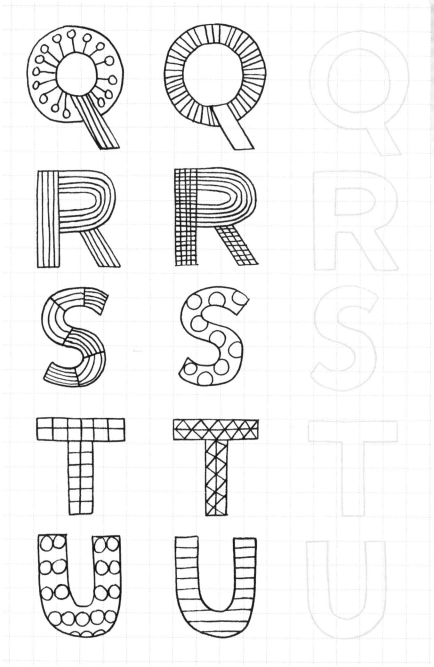

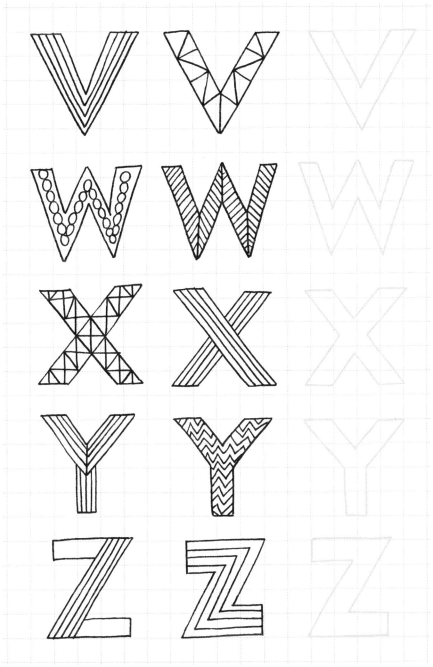

Decorate the leaves and color in.

Complete and add texture.

Add windows and doors.

Decorate
the vine
leaves.

EVERYTHING
BEGINS WITH
A DOT.

Wassily Kandinsky

Connect the dots to create a pattern.

Decorate with zigzags, spots, stripes, and checks.

Create your own butterflies.

Complete the geese.

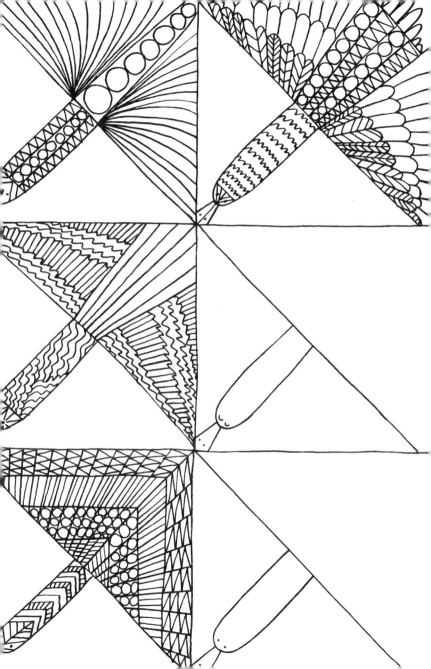

Complete the page.

Adorn the pots
with patterns.

Add patterns to the leaves.

Add windows and doors.

Complete the mice.

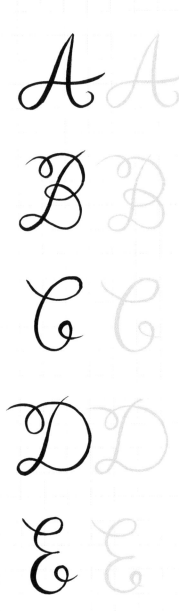

Here's a curly calligraphy exercise for you.

K K

L L

M M

N N

O O

Meditate

Quiet

Now

Tranquil

Relax

Practice your calligraphy by tracing these mindful words.

Add detail to the bear.

Tessellate.

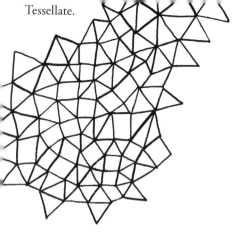

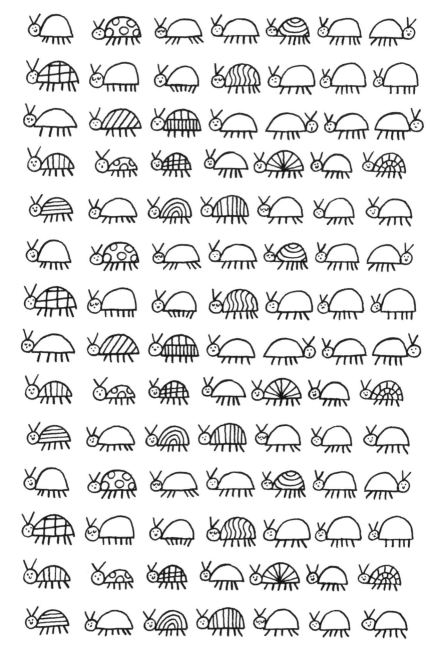

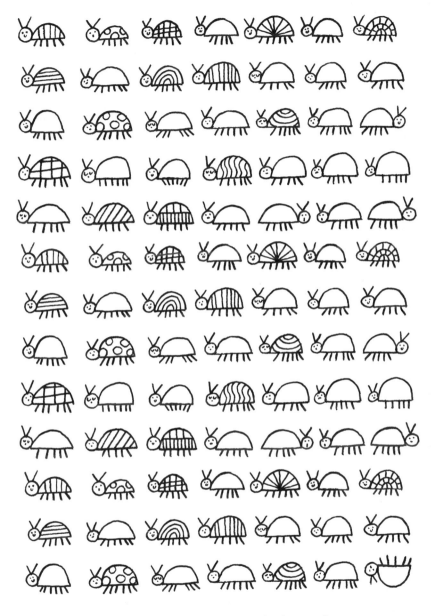

Some of these ladybugs need to be decorated.

Complete the butterfly.

THANKS

*To my two-year-old, Viggo, for reminding me
daily about the goodness of being present*

EMMA FARRARONS
illustration & art direction

emmafarrarons.com

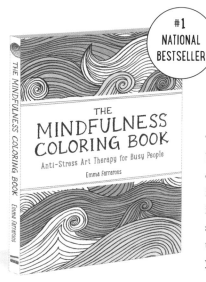

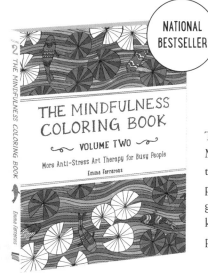

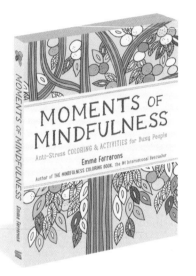